salmonpoetry
*Publishing Irish & International
Poetry Since 1981*

Equal Night
Graham Fulton

Published in 2017 by
Salmon Poetry
Cliffs of Moher, County Clare, Ireland
Website: www.salmonpoetry.com
Email: info@salmonpoetry.com

Copyright © Graham Fulton, 2017

ISBN 978-1-910669-88-4

All rights reserved. No part of this publication may be reproduced or transmitted in any form or by any means, electronic or mechanical, including photography, recording, or any information storage or retrieval system, without permission in writing from the publisher. The book is sold subject to the condition that it shall not, by way of trade or otherwise, be lent, resold or otherwise circulated without the publisher's prior consent in any form of binding or cover other than that in which it is published and without a similar condition, including this condition, being imposed on the subsequent purchaser.

COVER & TITLE PAGE IMAGES: Photograph of the aurhor's mother
AUTHOR PHOTOGRAPH: Iseult Timmermans
COVER DESIGN & TYPESETTING: *Siobhán Hutson*

Printed in Ireland by Sprint Print

*Salmon Poetry gratefully acknowledges the support of
The Arts Council / An Chomhairle Ealaoín*

To Helen,

and the memory

of Jessie

Acknowledgements

Some of these poems have been published before in the following magazines, anthologies and online journals:

New Writing Scotland 23: Queen of the Sheep, *Staple*, *Zed 2 O*, *Envoi*, *Poetry Nottingham*, *Fire*, *Pennine Ink*, *Word Riot* (USA), *Pennine Platform*, *Poetry Library at Southbank Centre website*, *Mind the Time*, *Hidden City Quarterly* (USA), *Chaparral* (USA), *Hospital Drive* (USA).

Contents

I

Messages	11
Think Positive	12
Side Effects	13
Monster	14
Changing Room	15
Heart-throb	16
Minute	17
Small Mercies	18
Views Described and Imagined	19
Relative	20
Big Screen	21
Cheer Up	22

II

Some Light	25
Skin	26
All	27
Impossible Sonnet	28
The Place	29
Equinox	30
Object	31
Before Our Time	32
Terrified	33
Refrain	34
Here's Looking at You Kid	35
Warm	36
Out There	37
Day Breaks Instead So You Hurry Home	38
Recycle	39
Ring Cycle	40

III

Services Rendered	43
Premonition	44
Part	45
Received	46
Here	47
D***h	48
Laugh	49
Sack Race	50
Space	51
Full Stop	52
Peace of Mind	53
Living Colour	54
Welcome to Resolution	55
This is Your Life	56
Precious	57
Soft Focus	58
Plastic Castle	59
About the author	60

I

Messages

I open the front door, hear you say
Blood in the urine . . . I've had a few tears . . .
I'll face it the only way I can,
the only way I understand.

The telephone line. Umbilical friend.
A private exchange not meant for me,
not just yet, not like this.

I muddle the weekend shopping on shelves:
bread and butter, dairy produce,
toothpaste, washing powder, milk,
daily survival, granted things.
The pulse in the wrist. Sun in the eye.

An episode of Corrie creeps by.
I ask you if there is something wrong.
You tell me of the blood, the tears,
the way you will face it, all of the tests
they'll hurry to do, decisions to make.
You tell me that I've not to worry,
wait and see what the doctors find.

Signals pounding around the brain.
Steam train heartbeat amplified.

An episode of Corrie creeps by.
Your thoughts have gone beyond the screen,
further than they've ever been.

Think Positive

Quiet cancer clinic corridors.

Nods of acknowledgement, fragile smiles.
Factsheets on tumours are fixed to the walls.
An untouched magazine choice on a table:
OK!, *HELLO!*, *The People's Friend*.

It's your turn next for radiotherapy.
Jessie is called. You pass from my gaze.
I hear you laughing along with the nurses,
chatting and laughing, it's what you do.

A block for your head to keep it still.
A whoosh of rays from a space-age lamp.

Isn't technology wonderful mum?

I came here today to ease your weight,
to help you believe you're never alone.
Instead it is me that feels alone;
how can I possibly reach what you see?

Heel-click echoes, sick people smell.

And here you are, finished again.
Lean on my arm, look at my face.
Radiant energy, half-minute blasts.
Isn't it great what they do these days?

Across the tearoom and biscuit bar.
One step, then one step. The pace
of aloneness. Partick sun.
The car is there to take you home.

Side Effects

You're happy your hair is not falling out.
This only happens with chemo, we're told.
That would be too much to bear –
having to wear a wig, be bald.

Strands in the basin. Clumps in your hand.
People staring, glancing away.

The radiotherapy isn't so bad,
all that you get is incredibly tired.
No throwing up too, your face in a mess.
You're spared all that; just lucky, I guess.

Monster

The sudden implosion of humdrum worlds,
safely flowing from night to day,
asleep to awake, awake to asleep,
replaced with dizzy, churning dread.
Dread is the only word that fits.
    A silence,
ferociously, patiently, growing
into our bones, a Quatermass ghost.
        It's not even evil, a villain to loathe,
something I can blow to bits,
something I can kill with a stake.
I can't even see it, can't even touch.
It's only doing its conscienceless job,
        dividing cells, efficient shit.
Shit is the only word that fits.

Changing Room

You say that you can't feel the floor anymore.
You say it's like trying to walk on a sponge.
The bathroom carpet's a sea on the moon.
You fumble your way. You're turning to air.
Or maybe you have no place anymore
for physics and theories, Dettol, Cif,
as gravity, tenderly, eases its hold
on all that you know. The soap. The plug.
The skindust layers. The water. The sink.
Your face in the mirror is vagued by steam.
You rub a small hole to check you're still there.

Heart-throb

A pint-sized rugby playing-type doctor
in ill-fitting jeans and rugby top
takes us into his office and gives us the lowdown.
Drop-kicks from the hip, tells it how it is.

No pussyfooting. No poetry.
No beating about the metaphorical bush.

He's a hard-tackling scalpel-wielding saviour
in the sinbin of life. There's a Clooney screen-saver
on his p.c., handsome and dashing in ER days.
The routes to existence a mouse-click away.

He, the surgeon, asks me if
a) I'm prepared for the probabilities
b) there's anything I want to ask.

There's nothing. You see, I know
everything will be just fine because
a) this only happens to other people
b) this only happens on TV shows.

Minute

Five past nine, first in line,
sterile theatre, save your life,
so we are told, nil by mouth,
across the city, happening now,
insert the needle, counting backwards,
four three two, blades and organs,
scrubbed-up doctors, save your life,
cancer dragon, shall be slain,
permission forms, the dotted lines,
will be done, no more choice,
except for one, sit, do nothing,
have you for a short while longer,
months, forever, rooms
                         of time,
and watch you live a hard cold death,
watch you going until you're gone,
your flesh, dissolving, transformation,
nothing is wasted, under your arm,
breaking your ribs, pacing the carpet,
swirling movie, conscious, stream,
runaway brain, projecting every
action they take inside
                         my head,
scalpel, cut, red and blood,
just last night, before we left,
you promised you would be a brave girl,
gave a thumbs-up, asked for a hug,
everything soon would be alright,
everyone, soon, will save your life,
so we are told, seven miles,
across the river, first in line,
happening, now, six past nine.

Small Mercies

Clean machines. Monitors, bleeps.

Seen-it-all nurses, sensible tights.
Streamlined hair, intensive care.

The surgeon has done his daily tour.
He's very pleased you're fighting hard.
Attitude is half the battle.
Courage, faith, can save the day.

The girlfriend of a comatose boy
clutches his hand and begs his name.
He banged his head while doing his job,
he probably won't wake up again.

His mum and dad have nipped for a fag —
down at the exit, same as the entrance,
taking a break from cradling his fate.

It's such a shame, a nice young lad
is what you'd say if you could speak.

An angel for every pristine sheet.

You've opened your eyes.
You're still alive.

Views Described and Imagined

Evening visit. Western Infirmary.
Trauma Unit. Level 8.
The slowest lift in all the world.
The slowest lift, in all the world.

Your ward room has a glorious view –
the soot-smudged tower of Glasgow Uni
licked by mid-September sun.

The previous scene was even better –
Clydeside cranes like Martian machines;
War of the Worlds, an unexpected,
crimson, cloudless, stripped-down sky.

You have to depend on me to report
the things you need to know are there.
Six billion lives just like before,
no one bothering all that much.
The TV in your room doesn't work,
all that you get is the video screen.
A Perfect World with Kevin Costner.
Sands of Iwo Jima, John Wayne.

A patient in an opposite bed,
out of her box, lost in space,
is wailing *Danny! Danny! Where are you?*,
seeing us from another place.

Another place, sounds quite nice.
A perfect world, sounds quite nice.

They'll shut her down
when it's time to sleep.
No one bothering all that much.

Relative

The sleep of *before* is, quietly, gone.
        The rhythm of Normal
  has turned and curved
to soothe the searing flash of knowing
it can't return, unruined, again.
Our sanity bends to take the strain
    of hurtling inside the new mundane,
the frightening currents of unknown, time.
Whatever is *then* is light years away.
The clock on the wall just softens, falls.
    When you look at a star
you're travelling through pain.

Big Screen

I ask you if it's alright if I go ten minutes early
because we're playing Germany tonight
in a make-or-break qualifier
and I'd like to make the Big Screen kick-off
in the Big Screen kick-off pub
with a big selection of beers on tap,
and you say *Of course son*
and *I hope your team wins*
and *I'll see you tomorrow.*
And Scotland are losing and the pub is full
of people I'll eventually never see again
and the screen is veiled by slow grey smoke
and a laughing German
is escorted from the premises,
and it's all increasingly small
and I can't really make you out
as I think of you alone in your head
and I wish I could have those ten minutes back.

Cheer Up

You've got a pretty face, my dear,
but if you can't cheer up, just a little,
maybe it's time for a new career.

You say this to a scunnered trainee
who's bored and blonde and thinking about
a boyfriend's kiss, a boyfriend's cock.
Pissed-off with catheters, hospital corners,
coffin dodgers, bedpans, sad.

She takes the huff and sashays right out.
The fluids are moving within the tubes.

What can that old bag ever know?
She was never young, like me,
she was never in love, like me.
She's never felt the way I feel.

Counting the minutes until her shift
is over, grabbing her mobile, running
down the steps, along the lane
for new sensations, ecstasy, laughs.

The futures are moving within the dark
to meet you, both, routine death.

What will the end of life be like?
The end of loving, being loved.
What can that young nurse ever know?
She was never old, like me.

II

Some Light

Checking your Bank of Scotland statement.
Marking the debits, adding, subtracting,
codes and credits, trying to grip
the biro, keep your self joined up.

The hours defined by packs of wipes,
antibiotics, disposable bowls.
The arms of nurses to lift you out
and lift you back into bed again.

Too cold, hot. Too dull, bright.
Carrying plastic chairs from the stack.
Kissing your forehead, holding your hand,
carefully ticking your tasteless meals.

Forgetting to ask what you love about life,
what you believe and what you have found,
what you wish you had done that you didn't.
Where you are going. Enlightenment.

Kissing your forehead, releasing your hand.
Returning the plastic chairs to the stack.

Skin

How little we know of those we love
behind the skin, how little
we show.
        A lorry empties the bloody bins.
        A burst of steam from the pipes outside.
I know I won't ever guess you at all.
Too shallow, too quick. On we go,
hold my words, it's never this late.
        An ambulance comes and leaves again.
Sitting beside ourselves in the dark.

All

Cold rice pudding spooned from a tub
into your old lady's baby mouth.
Full of nutrition, safe to give.
Nothing that's chewy or crunchy's allowed.

Ambrosia's very nice
and can give you the strength to help you fight
the thrush that's grown on your tongue and throat –
a side effect of the drugs they fed
to zap the infection deep in your chest.

This is all I can do for you.
Facing death with half-price desserts,
a Kleenex bib to catch all the drips.
This is what you did for me.
Hazy time-filled years, a breath.
It all comes back to where it begins.

Nine soft swallows, then you are done.
Did that feel good? You nod, smile,
strap the noisy mask to your face,
return your head to its pillow dent.
You tell us you're ready to rest for a while.

Impossible Sonnet

In a dream, you are taking your first determined step
helped by heaven-blessed nurses at the side of your bed
and playing *Beautiful Dreamer* on the hospital piano
as everyone claps and cheers and realises
that it's going to be okay after all and everything
is going to be just great for the rest of your life
and there will be no more operations, and pain.
Suddenly, you are driving a jump-on-the-back
room-for-one-more *Dead of Night* London bus
like a new born woman with one leg sticking out
of the cabin window as you career around a corner
taking all of eternity to turn and turning in a split-
second simultaneously as you balance miraculously
on two wheels even though you never learned to drive.

The Place

Rain. The rain. The window.
The rain.

A hospital rain is the cruellest of rains —
it washes our selfish certainties clean,
our flesh of silt, complacent pretence.

The things in your bag. I sift them again.
You ask the question you asked me before,
three minutes before. *Is it all there?*
Yes.

A cloud of annoyance drags over my eyes.
You clock it at once, you don't miss a trick.
That wasn't so hard, now was it?
No.

I lost the place. Forgive me.
I'm lost.

You ask the question you asked me before.
You cough more phlegm, heavy and thick.
The rain. The window. The room.
Rain.

It dismantles each of our cosy facades,
lays us out bare, what we really are.
I try not to look. A hospital rain
is the kindest of rains.
I have to look.

Equinox

You'll soon be moved to another hospital
closer to home when the infection has left
and then you'll be sent home and we'll
have to get you a wheelchair and we'll
have to learn how to use the wheelchair
and we'll learn how to feed you and lift you
in and out of the bath and we'll learn how to
wipe your arse and learn how to be mothers
and learn how to make you see that you are
not a burden which is what you fear most of all
but have never been and will never be
and all around us is the day of equal night
and a door for our spirits that can open or close
and the moment to choose the night won't win.

Object

What's the purpose in trying to distil
my sight, thoughts, the objects of fear.
Stethoscopes, chairs, syringes, hope.
    Death's not real, it's just for life.
I watch the other patients' eyes.
I wonder if there's anything there
worth mentioning here, there's probably not.
There probably is, I don't really care.
Squirty soap, Lucozade, grapes.
    It's not for them, it's not for you.
It's something solid I have to extract,
unflinching essence I need to become.
    Bereavement leaflets, directions to wards.
No pity or point, directions to truth.

Before Our Time

We appear early. The roads were clear.
You're here in half light. Blinds are drawn.
Pillows are too high. Sheets are tight.
You're not prepared. You're somewhere else.
Your eyes are closed. You talk to yourself.
Hushed, but insistent. Weak, but in tune.
A wish, or a prayer, or a stubborn reply
to voices telling you   *let it go*.
There are lives to consider. Those you love.
Things you will say that remain unsaid.
And we wait, very slowly, until you know
that somebody else has entered this room.
I wash your teeth. It is all unsaid.
The tap is running. Flowers are in bloom.

Terrified

A diet of steroids, the shoved-in drip,
is altering what you feel, perceive.

A whispering woman, again, in a doorway.
A doorway where there is no door.

You tell us you've never been so scared,
doubting the core of your cherished sense,
believing the horror of leaving your mind.

Terrified is the word you use.

We try to explain it's only their drugs.
Hallucinations, trippy impostors.
Chemical cuckoos, unreal reals.

The cord of your gown, snaking, alive.
A patient, motionless, shape. A moth.

Then after some days it snaps into place.
You shake your head as if to proclaim
Frightened of what I don't understand,
how could I possibly be so daft?

Real unreals, realisation.
A tulip turning into a penguin.

Refrain

Jackets zipped. Waiting to go.
Feeling guilty, eyeing the clock.
Looking ahead to driving home,
hoping to feel no feelings at all.

Turn it off. No feelings at all.

Lights down low, forcing a smile,
leaving you on your own again.
Wanting to go. Wanting to stay.
Keep your chins up, Ha Ha Ha.

And then you start to sing a song.
A voice so clear. Uncertainty gone.
A silly Glaswegian ditty about
a family who are always together.

Ayeways thegither, aw the time.

Jessie, hoping to make us laugh.
All the time, no sadness at all.
The night before the last of your life.
Wanting to stay. Waiting to go.

Here's Looking at You Kid

You had a bad night on the night before.
You've had no sleep for two in a row.
We'll stay with you,
go home when it's dawn.

We've brought a flask and pieces to eat,
books to read and *Casablanca* –
one of your top ten favourite films.
We play it when all the visitors leave.

You balance the volume arrows yourself.
We watch you watch the titles and cast,
watch you as you detach, drift,
fixing on somethings ahead of our sight.

You blether a bit about Franchot Tone,
an actor who doesn't appear in the film.

A nurse swishes past. A blasé glance.
Bogart and Bergman part in the mist.
You probably know
we're right at the end.

Warm

You suddenly get hot. You pull off your shawl.
    The nurse says *She seems quite agitated tonight*.
We find a fan and switch it on. You cool down.
You fall asleep. Your right arm moves slowly
up and down. It looks like it is waving.
We watch your face. We watch your arm.
I pull off my shoes. We fall asleep.
The silence wakes us. We know, the silence wakes us.
We watch for the breath. It finally comes.
We watch for the next. We watch for the rise
and fall of your chest.
A ticking noise comes out of your mouth.
    The nurse says *Can you leave the room please*.
We leave the room. She closes the door.
The corridor is bright. The ward is dark.
Everyone else is asleep. We know, you are dead.
We wait for the nurse to tell us what we already know.
The nurse comes and tells us what we already know.
    The nurse says *I'm very sorry*.
I start to shiver and ask for my shoes.
We go and say goodbye. They've tucked you up.
You're still warm. We hold you. They need the bed.
We pack away your things. You're still warm.
We ask the nurse to take the ring from your finger.
She can't. Another nurse comes and does it instead.
As we go we notice the shawl on the floor
and put it into the bag.

Out There

A nurse tells us how to get out as fast as we can
and we go down in the lift and wander about
with no idea how to get out
and there is nobody anywhere to ask
and no unwinding string to help us go back
and no noise except for our footsteps
in the minotaur labyrinth corridors
beneath the harsh headache hospital lights
in search of a way out or a cleaner
or a porter or a whistling doctor to ask
if they know the way out to the car park
and the new air and fresh tarmac and stars
which we see on the other side of a Kafkaesque door
which we consider kicking open
because there's nothing else to be done
until we notice a stair we hadn't noticed before
and suddenly we're in Accident and Emergency
and there's a girl behind a curtain
who covers her breasts as fast as she can
and laughter and blood and stabbed people on chairs.

Day Breaks Instead So You Hurry Home

At red. Not talking. Waiting
                for the traffic lights
        to change.
    Byres Road is deserted.
Jakies and junkies have gone to their beds.

Eardrum-achingly quiet, until, sublimely,
        Time takes a cigarette, puts it in your mouth,
        you pull on a finger, then another finger,
        then your cigarette
strums from a tenement window.
                Then nothing.
A needle being removed.

The first concert I ever saw.
                May the 18th, '73.
My skull was a buzz for a couple of days,
the world was never as loud again.
                Funny, the things
        that go through your mind.
The things that go.
                Through your mind.

Dumbarton Road is deserted.
    Ziggy Stardust has gone to his bed.
At red. Not talking. Waiting
                for what cannot
change to change.

Recycle

Rewinding my tape of previous life.
The wheelies are out, an alarm is on,
the garden is at the end of the drive.
      Why has the end of the world not begun?
Why am I putting one foot in front
of the other, one foot in front
                      of the other.
Turning a key, opening curtains.
      How can *This* just be the same?
A video's in, the timer is on.
It's far too soon for Corrie, I think.
The *Radio Times* is in the bin.
The mirror is hanging beside the bath.
      It feels important, appears to reflect
a clue to finding the way to find out.
One step in front of   the other. One step.

Ring Cycle

Drowsy light. Mild, no rain.
Spaced around the kitchen table.
Just past dawn, drinking whisky,
nearly a litre, little effect.
Zonked and warm, the shivering gone.
Mister Whyte and Mister Mackay.

The ring in the middle, a tiny shine,
easy to lose, slipping away,
rolling across the spotless floor
until it has reached the speed it needs
to blink into a different nowhere,
thoughtless energies, wiped of form.

Waiting for a reasonable hour
when people will be up and about,
filling the kettles, reading the papers,
Herald or *Record*, coffee or tea.

Beginning the list of telephone calls,
breaking gently, saying the news,
saying the same things over and over.
Very sudden. Very peaceful.

Tiny lives, easy to lose
sight of what is most important:
cats miaowing, rolling ahead
to what comes next, the speed we need.
Spaced around the kitchen table.
Drowsy light. Mild, no rain.

III

Services Rendered

Parlour. Soft talk. Gloom-coloured suite.
Leaflets with taste and up-to-date costs.
Booking the slot. Bury/burn?
Minister's bung, newspaper space.

Sad-dipped backroom. You in a box, the one
we picked from the catalogue choice.
Eyes. Shut. Glasses. Straight.
Isn't it great what they do these days?

Post-mortem cutting is hidden from view.
Prizing you open, reaching inside,
sealing you up, tagged and bagged.
Production line, it's best not to think.

Make-up, lip-stuff, not too much.
Hair done right, the way that you liked.
We gave them a picture, asked them if
they'd comb as close as they possibly could.

They did, it's you, a sculpture in ice.
We're fried in shock, saying goodbye
to something that is already leaving
everything, us, that still clings on.

A hearseboy through an open door gap
relaxing inside the admin office,
chilling before the next wee job.
Blowing on coffee, flicking a mag.

Premonition

As I try not to think of the autopsy scar
visible close to your neck
I remember how scared you were
because the surgeons
had come into your room
in the middle of the night
with masks over their faces
and instruments in their hands
to tell you they weren't finished with you yet,
and you were
going under the knife once more.

And we promised it was only a bad dream,
and all the operations were over,
and even asked a doctor to come in and reassure you,
which he did.

Part

The deathmen in step. The catafalque.
The synchronised shoulders,
rehearsed respect.

The sound of shoes,
a well-oiled withdrawal.
The coffin is on the catafalque.
Your all-alone body is lying inside.

Your music is played. The prayers are prayed.
I clumsily mumblingly murder your hymns.
The coffin begins,
the coffin is gone.

We don't need to see you
to know you are gone.

A silently audible hum of machines.
The catafalque is as it was.
Incinerator. Grinding room.
All that is is as it was.

Received

The caterer has conjured a feast
of retro sandwiches and sausage rolls,
and we place your framed photo on a table
with an artificial flower to one side of it
and a dram of whisky to the other
for those who want to see you.
And I fork out the bill to a stooge in a suit
who saunters away to get a receipt,
and the room becomes less,
and the voices recede
to mud-shaped blurs,
and the emptiness is complete.

Here

Head-racing, unsleeping, unwanted light.
The glow from the digital radio-clock.

A vein of space separates the curtains.
Moonshine leaks its way inside,
projects a flickering film on the wall,
restless spirits of see-through white.

Familiar, ancient, malignant, sly.
Imagine how it feels to be dead -
nothing at all in nothing at all.

Deep-rooted fears. Primeval claws.

It's seconds like this the end of our lives
pads up behind me, taps my shoulder,
says *My child, the corner's here.*

I step out of bed and fiddle them shut.
The darkness is absolute, smothering-tight.
Singularity-black. No one comes back.

D***h

We mustn't ever talk about *it,*
or write about *it*, or face up to *it*.
The king of taboo, don't mention *that word*.
We have to slosh *it* down the pit,
keep things clean, comforting, neat.
        We mustn't ever confront the idea
that all we build amounts to zilch,
but keep on building anyway.
All we create will change to clouds,
        there is no God, no heaven hell.
All those Saints, it's just as well,
getting under each other's feet.
Angels with harps, demons with horns
        hopping about, bothered, hot.
Everything's for no reason. Pish.

Laugh

In the car on the road to the cemetery gate.

We've picked you up from the undertake shop.
A plastic maroon-coloured urn's on my lap,
the colour of Heart of Midlothian's strip.
A numbered sticker's been slapped on the lid.
You've changed to flakes of Scott's Porage Oats –
you'd laugh if you could see yourself.

The cemetery garden, high mossed walls.
Amongst the paraphernalia of grief:
butterflies, fairies, cherubs and chimes,
a frog with a cello, names in stones.
Angels and teddies and local team scarves –
you'd laugh if you could see yourself.

A looking glass gauze. A dislocation.

Dreamily soothing, a womb cocoon.
It takes us a while to tip you all out –
you'd laugh if you could see yourself.
Humpty Dumpty, together again.
A bottomless pot, that's all there is,
some of you hitches a lift on the wind.

Sack Race

A bin bag pyramid raised on your bed.
Twenty-one black sacks pregnant with clothes.
Sweaters, skirts, blouses, gloves,
cardigans, scarves, jackets, hats.

Food for the skips, the charity shops.
The Children, The Aged, Cancer Research.
Pairs of shoes, a lot no use,
everything cleared in two or three hours.

No sink in pause, no pit stop to think.
Laughing to stop ourselves going mad.
Fashion victims, phantoms of cloth,
a single shoe, its partner, gone.

The sacks are thin, we see right through.
Trousers, coats, nighties, tights.
Oxfam ghosts in a halfway house,
knickers, dresses, slippers, bras.

A penny for luck in every purse.
Kirby grips and tubes of pastilles,
Safeway receipts and books of matches,
three-ply tissues, unbroken seals.

A non-politically correct fur coat –
if anything should have been sacked it's this.
I haven't the heart, I picture your face.
A single shoe found under the bed.

Space

Air with no one to breath it is sad.
    I'm trying to see you no longer Are,
a voice, smile, a constant, voice.
Someone I can say *Goodbye* to,
someone I can walk around.
    Fingers, belonging, a human, home.
The three piece suite could do with a clean.
Depending on the ordinary things.
    They say *It will ease*. I'm sure it will.
I don't understand you've stopped being You.
Half in sun

    and half in cold.
    Happiness, presence, movement, touch,
remembrance, kindness, atoms, mass.
    Most of an atom is made up of space.
A space with no one to cross it is sad —
moving from here to   here
to here. Someone who has given birth,
someone I can cradle to sleep.
      The fish van blasts its once-a-week horn.
    The *is*ness you used to fill is loud.
Words with no one to mean them are dumb.

Full Stop

Baby, I Don't Care.

A biography of Robert Mitchum
deserted on your bedside table.
Smirking, carelessly, cool, on the cover.
Ava Gardner watching his face.

The bookmark trapped at page 64,
or 65, I'll never know
the very last word you saw before
your eyes got tired, you placed it down.

The ultimate punctuation mark.
Comma, colon – I don't suppose
it's very important, it's only scratches,
head-fuddled memory, soft back pulp.
Nothing that proves you were even here;
dimensions outside the film in my brain.

A lamp, a half-vanished bag of mints,
hairs on a hairbrush, prints on a phone,
dust-fur on the out-of-work bulb.
The very last world whenever you left.

RIP. Processing a need.
A pressy for Christmas, less than a year.
Somebody dead to read all about.
£8.99 RRP.

Peace of Mind

An odyssey on
                a rain-pelted street.
Each old lady I see is you.
Pavement,
        bank,
post office,
      shop.
My head is seduced by songs of death.
Tomorrow is drifting further,
                        out.
The oceans around
my pieces of mind.
You have to come
                and talk to me,
tell me there's nothing
                we still have to say.

Living Colour

In a drawer among the courting letters library cards
ration books gift tags christening cards
is a brooch in the shape of a lizard
the same one in my favourite photo
with dad nearest the camera at your right shoulder
and gran at your left shoulder and great-gran
at her left shoulder the furthest beyond of all
with you smiling always into our eyes
with your comfy coat and cheap brooch
which has outstayed all these travellers
with their eggshell days of hoping and trying
and moving to something that they have no fear of
although I didn't even know it was red until I saw it
a second ago it was always black and white.

Welcome to Resolution

In a dream, I'm waiting to meet someone
at the reclaim carousel of a terminal
I don't recognise in a place I've never been to,
and the arrivals are coming towards me
then going on beyond me with eager faces
like the perfect energy of restless water
that's been there before memory was invented,
and I'm still waiting when I see you
a little to the right and moving on beyond
although I'm probably remembering all wrong,
and I look at you and say *Mum, you're not dead
after all*, even though we both know you are,
have always been, will always be, and you
don't say anything at all and let me
lead you to a chair and sit you down
while I carry on searching for whoever I'm here for.
And when I turn to look at you again your face
gently melts and becomes the face of someone else
and I never do find out who I was meant to meet.

This is Your Life

A red-covered album, full of snaps.
We put it together for your birthday.
70, 1999.

All of your life, or what we could find:
work, wedding, babies, pram.

Images of your mother and father,
images of the children you had.
Holding us safe inside your coat.
Winter Sundays, waiting for dad
to catch a fire, shovel the ashes,
match the twisted papers and coals.

We gave you the book,
you went out dancing,
came back home, plugged in the fire,
wore an I AM 70 badge.

And now you're a name on a cemetery wall,
a photograph tacked to a cloister plaque.

Yet what remains is so much more
than bags of Get Well, Sympathy cards.
I see you walking along the Drive
concentrating on watching your feet,
a gift of advice to keep from falling,
something your granny used to believe.

It's all true. You'll always be.
Unfallen, warm, inside us, safe.
This beat, then this beat.

Precious

I remember, suddenly, the gold stain
that appeared on a summer's evening
on the brand new rug that you loved.
And we took turns at trying to lift it out
with none of us owning up
as you took a fit, and dad sat in silence
with *Songs of Praise* in the background.
And we scrubbed, rubbed and hammered
with suds and water, and watched
with rising disbelief as nothing, nothing
had the slightest effect until, suddenly,
as quietly as it had appeared, the gold
winked out, and we saw
it had only been a patch of sun, only
a leaf of light, a trick, and we laughed,
and it was never ours to destroy or create.

Soft Focus

A little girl and a man
paddling. He wears a white
shirt and pullover.
White baggy trousers
rolled up above the ankles.
He holds the girl's hand.
The distance is around them.
Both look at a tiny white
yacht at their feet.
The moment is behind you.
A cigarette between the first
and second fingers of his
left hand.

Plastic Castle

Memory, tracks. I keep turning back.
A toy shop castle you gave me for Christmas.
Battlements, drawbridge, a magical sight.
I played with it twice or, possibly, once.

Memory bank. Child-friendly knights.
A hard-earned gift you gave me for Christmas,
when I was seven, or eight, or six.
I'm not too sure. I hope I said thanks.

Scottish poet GRAHAM FULTON was born in 1959. He's been published widely in magazines, anthologies, newspapers and online journals in both Europe and the USA, and his many books of poetry include *Humouring the Iron Bar Man* (Polygon, 1990), *Knights of the Lower Floors* (Polygon, 1994), *Full Scottish Breakfast* (Red Squirrel Press, 2011), *One Day in the Life of Jimmy Denisovich* (Smokestack Books, 2014), *Photographing Ghosts* (Roncadora Press, 2014) and *Brian Wilson in Swansea Bus Station* (Red Squirrel Press, 2015). He's co-author of *Pub Dogs of Glasgow*, *Pub Dogs of London* and *Pub Dogs of Manchester*, all published by Freight Books. He was a contributor to an anthology of translated Palestinian poetry called *A Bird is Not a Stone* published by Freight in 2014, and he's also published over 20 pamphlet collections, many of which combine poetry, photography and illustration. He runs Controlled Explosion Press and lives in Paisley.